ZEUS
— AND —
HIS BROTHERS

CHILDREN'S GREEK & ROMAN MYTHS

BABY PROFESSOR

EDUCATION KIDS

A myth is a traditional or legendary story about strange beings and heroes, but are also about understanding the world. Some stories are magical and do not have a natural explanation. Most stories have gods and mythical creatures.

The ancient
Greeks told
stories about
their Gods.
These stories
are called
myths.

The magical
world of
the ancient
greece
was full of
fights, wars,
fear, fun,
adventures,
punishment
and love.

Zeus,
poseidon, and
hades were
the three sons
of cronos.

Zeus ruled the
sky and was
the king of all
the gods.

He had many
powers. He
could throw
thunderbolts
and change
his shape to a
human or an
animal.

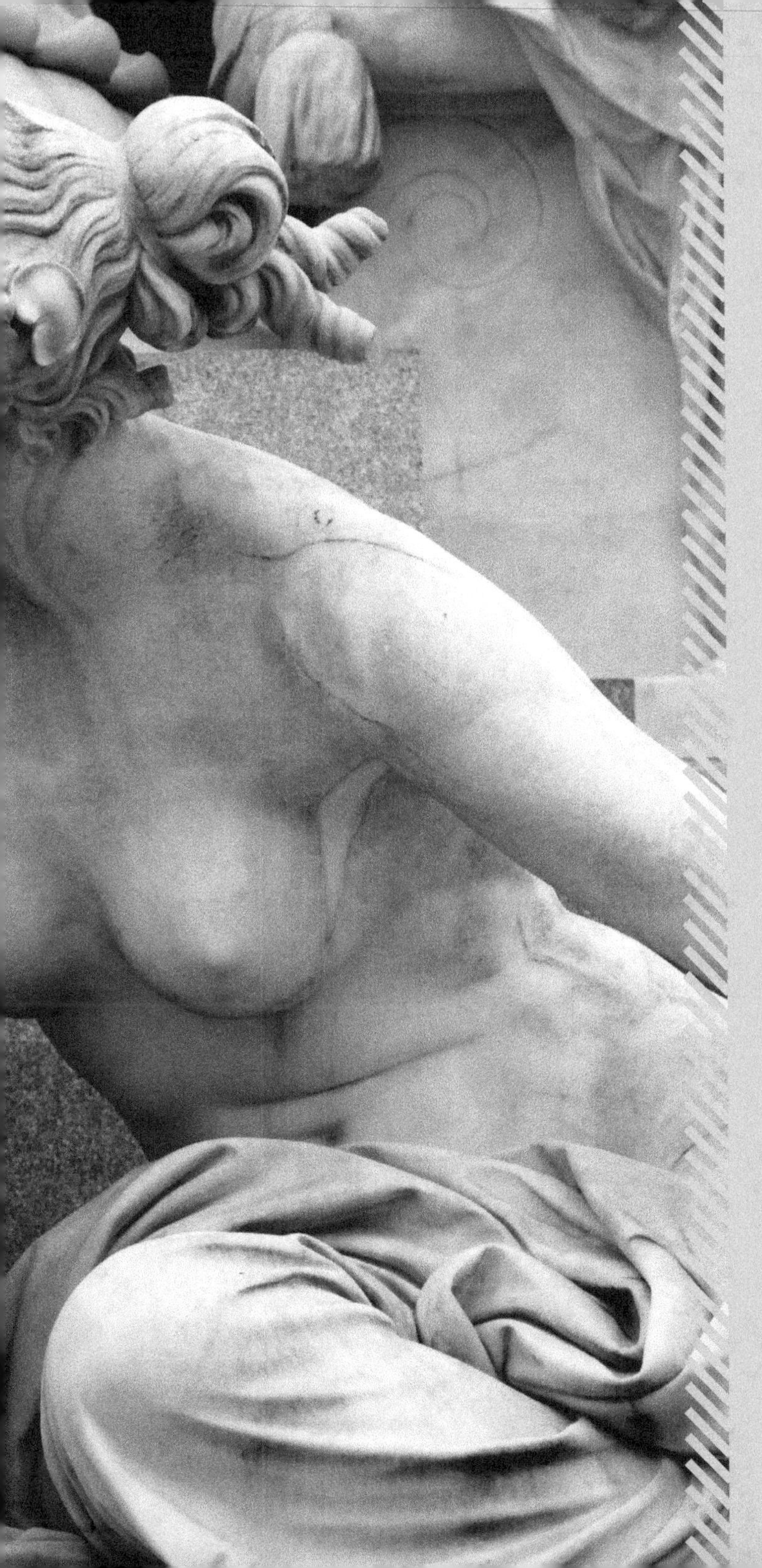

Zeus married Hera. Hera was the queen of all the gods, and also the goddess of marriage. She was zeus' sister. Zeus truly feared his wife.

Poseidon
was the
brother
of zeus.
Poseidon
ruled over
the rivers
and the seas.

Poseidon was
very happy
being lord
of the sea.
He had deep
blue eyes and
streaming
green hair.

He was
impatient
and powerful.
He could
magically
create an
island or send
a huge tidal
wave with a
wave of one
hand!

Hades
ruled the
underworld.

Hades was
not the lord
of death. His
job was to
run things
down in the
underworld.

The ancient
greeks
believed
that the
underworld
was the place
where people
go after
death.

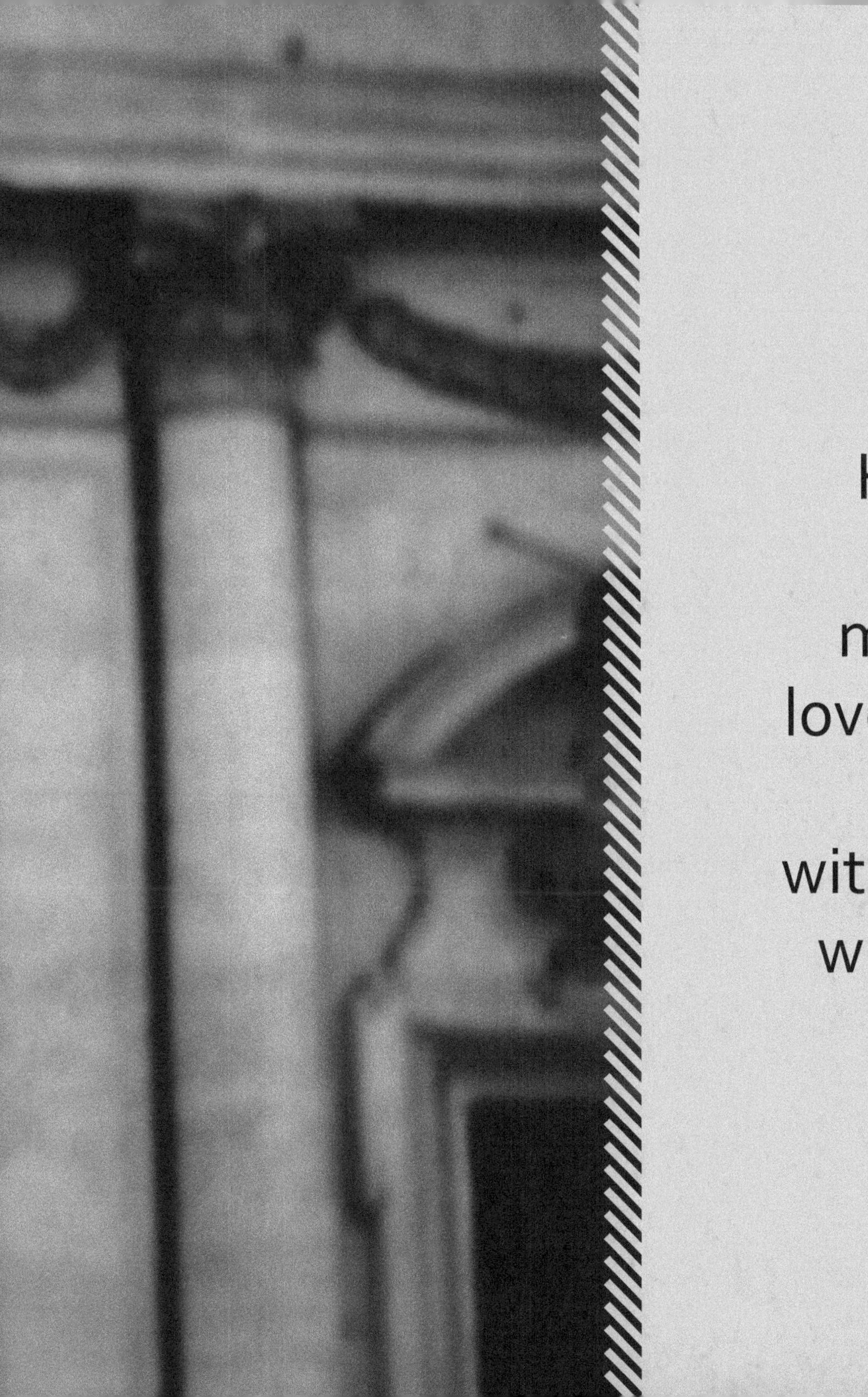

Hades was
a gloomy
man but he
loved to play,
especially
with toys and
with his dog
cerberus.

Roman
mythology is
a collection
of traditional
stories, beliefs
and rituals.

Romans used
mythology
to describe
the origin
of roman
civilization,
culture,
history and
religion.

The story of
the founding of
Rome is a well-
known myth.
It describes
twin brothers,
Romulus and
Remus, born
to a woman
named Rhea
Silvia and the
roman god of
war, Mars.

Roman
mythology
was strongly
inspired
from greek
mythology.

Jupiter was considered the king of gods and god of thunder and lightning. He was also the patron god of rome and was the roman version of the greek god Zeus.

Legends of Hercules (son of Jupiter), The Sixth Roman King Sirvius, Lucretia, horatius at the bridge, and Cybele are an important part of roman mythology and folklore.

There are more to know about Zeus and his brothers. Research and have fun!

Visit

BABY PROFESSOR
EDUCATION KIDS

www.BabyProfessorBooks.com

to download Free Baby Professor eBooks and view
our catalog of new and exciting Children's Books